THE
DEATH
CYCLE
MACHINE

Shadow and Light
Two Blocks Apart
An Easy Life
Home Fires
Goin' to the Chapel

THE DEATH CYCLE MACHINE

POEMS

Charlotte Mayerson

CROWN PUBLISHERS, INC.   NEW YORK

Published by Crown Publishers, Inc., 201 East 50th Street, New York, New York 10022. Member of the Crown Publishing Group.

Random House, Inc. New York, Toronto, London, Sydney, Auckland CROWN and colophon are trademarks of Crown Publishers, Inc.

Manufactured in the United States of America

Design by June Bennett-Tantillo

Library of Congress Cataloging-in Publication Data

Mayerson, Charlotte, 1927–
The death cycle machine / Charlotte Mayerson. —1st ed.
    p.   cm
1. AIDS (Disease)—Patients—Poetry. 2. Mothers and sons—Poetry. 3. Death—Poetry. 4. Grief—Poetry. I. Title.
PS3563.A9553D43   1996
811'.54—dc20
95-30618
CIP

ISBN 0-517-70279-7

10 9 8 7 6 5 4 3 2 1

First Edition

For
Robert Henry Mayerson
August 15, 1954
January 2, 1990

CONTENTS

THE
DEATH
CYCLE
MACHINE

LAYOUT

I didn't consider
When I chose your name
How it would look
On a tombstone.

THE WOMEN OF
THE HOLOCAUST

Without the women of the Holocaust
Who saw their children ripped asunder
I could not go on.
Without the women
Of eighteen hundred and five
Who bore eight children and raised five
I would go under.
Without my grandmother
Who had thirteen
And lost three—
As a young mother, she lost three—
Without all those unnatural women
Who, like me,
Let themselves fall out
Of their own place
In the natural order,
Who, because they could not
Save their young—
Hide them in a safe place—
Became outlaws,
Grave transgressors
Of natural laws,
Without those women
Before my eye I would die now—
In the right order—
While he's still alive.

GLAD I DIDN'T
WASTE MONEY

Glad I didn't waste money straightening that tooth
Glad I resisted
Though they warned
The misalignment
Would cause wearing away,
Decay,
By the time he was middle-aged.
Well, at least I don't have to worry about *that*.

"Did I tell him everything he needs to know?"
When he left home
(Left home. At the very least.)
I sewed name tags
On all his clothes
With stitches so tiny
They were like a thousand stored penances
To the account of that question.
Well, whatever he doesn't know
Doesn't matter now, does it?
That's a relief.

(And the shirt I chose to bury him in?
That blue and white checked job he wore to death?
Unmarked.
Never mind, no laundry service where he's gone
     now.
Losing stuff is no problem

That's for sure.)

"My God! I forgot about the earlobes—
Or the toes."
I'd prod myself with those
When I was pregnant
As if not attending them
Might mean he didn't get them
Or got imperfect ones. . . .
And maybe there was something to it.
Toward the end, he said,
"AIDS has cured me of athlete's foot."
Thank God we don't have that to deal with
     anymore.

Or his eyes.
His grandfather had glaucoma
So I'd nag him
To get his eyes checked.
He went blind anyhow—
Not from glaucoma, though,
That wasn't the problem I'm happy to say.

Though he didn't die of lung cancer
He did stop smoking
There's that to be thankful for
And though he was always climbing

To the top of the tallest tree
And going on wild adventures
To places I'd never even heard of . . .
He escaped all that.

Because he was so carefully brought up,
He was safe.
Such dangers didn't touch him.
There's that to take comfort in.

Of course when he was thirty-five
The bogeyman got him anyhow.
Test score? Zero.
That's the very thing
So-called mothers
Are meant to prevent.

WHATEVER ELSE

Whatever else is going on,
Autumn leaves underfoot sound
Like biting into a hundred jelly apples
Or cracking the crust
Of newly frosted November puddles,

Or a windy morning above the Hudson,
The sun a bright white,
The sky high for New York,
The fallen leaves dervishes
Whose rustle
The children mimicked, whirling,
Casting their own confetti
Into the restless air.

(Lying on the grass,
The sharp breeze
A love-scratch on my cheek,
I told myself: "Remember this.
This is happy.")

Or years later,
As my son's rolling chair
Flattened the red and yellow
Windfall on the country lawn,
The sardonic crackle
Of wheels crushing

Dried out vegetation.

(He asked for a leaf
And then sweetly,
Lightly,
Trailed his finger
Over his last Fall.)

Today,
Patti's newly nursed baby
Stretched out on my lap,
I lightly
Trail my finger
Over the taut, pink belly
And hear only
A juicy summer content.

HAIKU FOR
AN EAST ASIAN
SCHOLAR

I didn't teach you to ride
A two-wheeled bike
That summer
So you could die.

THE DEAD SEEP

The dead seep so cold around me
My underpinnings numb
It's hard to keep my footing
But a fall
Fast entombs me
Within the solid wall
Of their now upright
And frozen number
Whose thick ice
Muffles music
Thins out hue
Even your ardent hand
Lacks the heat
To blast through
Only the stranger's bland
"Do you have any children?"
Is torch enough
To reach me.

LAST CALL

I've been too long on the wrong side
Of cliffs that claw the sky
And hurl oiled flanks down on the seas
For these teasing colloquies.
Too long my passage a cat-walk
To mark the pace of graceful talk
The orchestrated clue . . .
And you,
Here at last
Where we may give this fast
Pulsing, deadly game
Its own bare name,
I beg you. Compel
Your subtly veiled eyes,
Hurry.
Uncover.
Look, who can tell?
We may here see each other.

ETIQUETTE FOR FORMAL OCCASIONS

Aunt Mary died at sixty-three
Her dignity on burial marred
By a dark stain
On the bright sunlight:
My grandmother,
Both hands lifted—
Palms up—
As if catching rain
Or like a graveside panhandler
Slowly working the half circle
Of the congregation,
Keening at us,
"Think of the mothers!
Think of the mothers!"

I almost leapt at her
So unseemly it was
And, after all,
It was poor Mary
Down in that hole.

The hell with seemly.
I seek now the alms she sought
When the begging bowl
Of her cracked hands
Thirsted for other people's tears,
For watery prisms
A mother could hold up
To fracture the black rock
Of a child's death.

BIBLE STORY

Oh my son, Absalom,
Would God I had died for thee,
Oh Absalom, my son, my son.

Absalom? Who killed his brother?
Seized his father's throne?

Ah, but even in his dotage
David could say where justice lay:
The first crime, the fruit of Tamar's rape.
David preferred that no one pay
That, unavenged,
The girl just slink away.
The second crime, no crime.
It was not David alone
Who could count the ways
He'd shamed himself.
Absalom kept such careful note
He also could tote up
Who deserved the throne.

And think of how he died,
Absalom,
His hair caught in the limb
Of a terebinth tree,
Three of Joab's darts in his heart.
(Joab, who imagined loyalty

Proved him the king's true progeny.)

Now think of your own son, hanging
In a turpentine tree,
You ready to cede your life,
Your kingdom to him,
And those self-righteous bastards . . .
What do they know?
Nothing.
Nothing about a king
And his son.

And to kill him like that!
Imagine it.
Imagine what your own beautiful boy
Looked like, hanging there
In a terebinth tree,
The bitter fruit of a turpentine tree.

It was with poisoned darts
They stabbed my son
And, like they did with Absalom,
Hacked pieces off him.
Imagine it.
To do such a thing
Before his heart stopped.

THE DEAD WATCH OVER US

What's wrong? "I can't lie down."
Why not? "I fell again."
Where? "On Forty-second Street."
On Forty-second Street?
"So," he wants to know,
"Would it be nicer to do
On Park Avenue?"
Smart ass.

I plummet into bottomless sleep,
Can't find my home room,
Board the wrong train,
A steel ramp
Relentlessly tumbles me
Back where I started
Until, rewired like a new mother
To her babe, a faint gasp
Makes me leap to his bed,
Pummel his back,
Prop up his head.
"Tea," he whispers,
"Let's try tea."

Only that necessity
Could drag me down the hall,
Hand trailing the wall
For the rest stops
Impending doorframes provide.
(Last year, when my pretty little mother
Was dying in that room—
It's our dying room—
She measured half a block
From bed to kettle
And warned the wall would smudge,
Trailing your hand like that.)

It's ten degrees outside
But so fetid, so thick, the sickness
Inside, I crack the window,
And by that time
Need something fine
To unsnag the creeping vine
Caught in my spine.
Now, just sliding under the Big Red,
I remember the still-open window
By his bed.
Flow gently, sweet Afton,
Disturb not his head.

Yet in the only bed I can find
Lies not my child, but my father
With his look of a chieftain:
"A prince," my mother said,
Hand soft on his coffin,
"He was always like a prince."

Not in this place.
Here, his nose has decomposed
A chalky decay soils his cheek.
I shriek at him until it rips my throat,
Daddy, Daddy,
You never listen to me!
Never!
Robert's so sick
And you do
Nothing to help us.
Nothing!"

My lies slice the air
To seek and destroy his heart.
"No, no, please," comes the dear old voice,
"I beg you . . .
I always listen to you, sweetheart."

I'm wild now
To find my child

To jam the window tight
Against the cold night . . .

But in this new lemon-lit room
There are only empty beds
Covered with cracked and yellowing plastic.

There is no doubt:
Those who once lay in these beds,
The former patients,
All,
Are now dead.

GYPSY QUESTIONS

It was milk that blinded me
When an angry gypsy
Bared her breast to bead me.
My mannerly father's response?
Hilarity. Falling-down laughter.
My father, you see, loved gypsies.

Unreliable?
"Not at all," he said.
"Year after year
They'd arrive at the vineyard
Just when the grapes were ripe,
Calling, 'The cousins are here!
Tap a barrel, bake the eggplant,
Roast the corn!'"

Disrespectful?
"Not at all," he said.
"They may be Jews
Who missed the wagon call
After the Red Sea bridge
Washed out.
The word gypsy after all
Does come from Egyptian."

And then his eyes—
So light they were almost white—

Would lose their focus.
"I used to dance with them,"
He'd murmur, "every year,
After the harvest was in."

Not even
The Holocaust's even hand
Made me own my redheaded father
Gypsy kin
But at his grave,
Locked in a spin,
I remember
How he loved to dance.

AND THEN THE
DOORBELL RANG

"And then the doorbell rang."
Ten times a day,
Circling in on a sound wave,
That phrase finds me.
Maybe it means rescue:
"Answer the bell, dummy,
A dark stranger's out there
Waiting to save you."

The dreambook says: "For a doorbell,
Play the number three seventy,
And if you push the bell gently,
You'll have stimulating adventures
With someone you love."

Though I'd never push the bell,
Just before the plague,
Rob and I did go to Burma,
To the plain of Pagán,
To Mandalay. In Rangoon
We sat in the banquet hall
Of the ruined Strand Hotel,
Stained pink tablecloths
Banners to the city's decay.
Day after day, stranded,

We ate fake lobster thermidor
To Rob's fake dialogue
After Graham Greene.

In the hospice, Sandra
My ever-so-slowly dying
Baby sister says,
"Explain something to me.
Ten times a day, I almost say:
'When the time comes,
I want to be turned over.'"
I don't know what that means
But when they begin to slide away
I try to glide smoothly beside them.
Sometimes, outside the sickroom
I hang warning signs:
Don't mention Christmas. It's July.
We're in Rangoon and Rob will soon
Take the dog out.

One day, when I bring him some water
He chirps, "Thanks,
It's for Grandma,"
And hands it into the air
Where I guess she flew
In nineteen eighty-two.

(Hold still. Wait until
He's deep asleep
To mop up the spill.)

On guard again with Sandra,
I sit in distaff Bible study,
Weaving commentary,
Unravelling the Word.
Hours pass until
To ease her fear
I slip her something
And murmur—oh, how can I?—
Murmur to the only living relic
Of my own life,
"Give in to it, sweetheart,
Give it a chance,
Let yourself rest awhile."

Despite the drug, the pain—
Alight with revelation—
She sits straight up,
"That's what it means,
That's the answer!
What you said:
Give in to it. Let myself rest,
Turn myself over
Now the time has come . . ."

She is in terror,
But, good Jew,
It gives her pleasure
To work it through.

Lately, I'm picking up a new message
Calm, steady:
"Charlotte . . . Charlotte . . . Charlotte . . ."
Are they all calling me? Maybe,
But it sounds like my own voice
And the expert of choice,
My brilliant son,
No longer deciphers messages.

Then turn to the dreambook:
The closest it comes to Charlotte—
Cheap shot—is Chocolate:
"If you dream of chocolate
You will go through an illness."
It's close enough.
What are you waiting for?
Play the number five thirty-four.

ANCHO Y AJENO

The world is wide and alien
And I side with those
Who roll to the edge
But would I rather have
A grandchild
Than my own child
Dead of AIDS?

TRAVEL SERVICES

We need help
Out in a rain
That flagellates
Corrodes
I in pink chiffon
Cut low
He so weak
He can't stand
Can't speak
(Remember Bogotá?
The rain so dense
We lost each other?)

I drag him to a Hilton hotel
Where no cab attends
And the only phone's outside
I will not take him out again
Sue me I will not.

Prop him in a chair
And tear out of there
In flimsy gown
I have to go to the bathroom.

A uniformed maid
Is using the phone
Tear back

To find Oh Christ
The lobby door locked
I see him there
Through clouded glass
In that cavernous room
Stiff in that chair
Among silent
Uncaring strangers
All of them old.

Tear back
Flash a ten dollar bill
The biddy nods
Palms the dough
But the talk rolls on:
"Well you know the Rogos"
She says into the phone
"That's what that family is like."

Who are those Rogos anyhow
To doom my child
To an antechamber
A holding room
I cannot storm?

Plate glass the door
Unbreakable

Where's the key?
Where's the lock?
I can't get to him
We need help
My hands are bleeding
I barely make him out
So stiff
In that chair
Where's the help?

AIDS IN THE HOUSE

This house don't need more testing thank you
This house was certified structurally sound
Even they could tell you that
From their own experience
For years now they've been tearing pieces off us
Throwing small bombs, stink bombs,
High-powered explosives,
That plastique stuff.

This house don't need no demolition crew
We've got our own built in.
Some of our inside people?
Specialists. Know how to do that kind of work
Or else who to call.

This house gave at the office
There's nothing left to give
And we've stopped explaining
The whole damn ball of wax—
Whatever that means—
No call to do that.
How come they can't figure it out for themselves?

This house,
The members of this household,
We just go along

Do what there is to do
What choice do we have?

In the meantime
We're camping out in our own house
Living here while we wait
With our shoes on, pants, even in bed.

"Let's go home
What are we waiting for?
I want to go home."

This is home, son,
Our house.
See that picture on the wall?
The I-V pump?
Your wheelchair?
See? It's all our things, dear,
Here in our own home.

"If this is home,
Then I want to go someplace else.
Call up those guys with the lead ball,
Let's get rid of this place
We're always hanging around in
MothermakemybedsoonImwearyand
fainwouldliedown."

Hear that?
This house don't need more lessons
There's a lot we know
Even teachers don't know.

Ease up on us for God's sake,
This house can't take another earthquake.
See? There's trembling going on here.
Come on. Don't be afraid. Put your hand out.
Here. Feel that?
That's a seizure.
It will take
Only one more killing shake like that

For this house to go down.

BURNT OFFERING

A young woman's clanging
Cymbal-banging screams
Set off the ward:
Down the hall an old man
Falls out of bed
And a hoarse
"Nurse!" "Nurse!"
"Nurse!"
"Nurse!"
"Nurse . . ."
Ticks out a fading coded signal:
Don't ignore me,
Let me lie here,
Die here on the floor
Untended,
Unwound,
"Nurse!"
"Nurse . . ."

Do not scream.
We do not scream.
My son
Has never once screamed
Never pitied himself
(Or me).

But how else remind them
I'm here too
Pain unzipped,
My own mother long dead,
The call bell just out of reach
Off the side of the bed?

Listen, You,
Hear my noble silence?
Observe my gallantry?
A burnt offering, this body,
Charred.
Hinénee,
Here am I,
Accept this sacrifice,
Turn Your blind eye
To this pyre,
Save him, Bastard.

EMERGENCY ROOM

His brain's inflamed?
Never mind.
The brave young intern,
Defying stroke,
Paralysis,
System shutdown,
Gallantly orders a spinal tap.
No skin off her back
And he's got AIDS after all.

"Do it and I'll sue,
Do you hear?
Not the hospital,
But you . . .
Personally."
I snarl it,
Then stand with arms,
As they say, akimbo,
Daring this bimbo
To touch him.

She threatens to call a guard,
I to call her mother.
Gauntlet down
We circle the gurney,
Fierce, wary,
Eyes on the prey

Until . . . the Lone Ranger arrives,
The Solon, the Chief,
And Judgement sounds:
"Contraindicated, Doctor."

In celebration
Rob raises the Coke I'd brought him
And, weakly sipping,
Before he chokes on mother love,
Grants me a single, bashful wink.

(You can look for
Such solace
If you like. We found
In the end
That partners in pain
Don't count for much.)

BEDSIDE COLLOQUY

He says:
"You're the kind of person
who makes even people you don't know
feel happy."

To me implying:
"Imagine how happy you make me feel,
your son,
whom you do know."

Except: He thinks he
is the people I don't know.
That is: right now,
when I'm the kind of person
who makes even people I don't know
feel happy ...
He doesn't know me.

Later: *"There's someone here*
pretending she's you,
said she was my mother,
gave your full name,
even your maiden name.
I mean, I may be sick
but I still know
my own mother ...

don't I?"

A WALK AT TWILIGHT

This time
They've angled a mirror
Across the road
To hurl at me
A heron-legged girl
In satin shorts
Wheeling, one-handed,
A sandy haired boy of three.
As if confetti showers
Fêted their way—
Smiling, cool,
Long eyes straight ahead—
They sashay past
A fine old plane tree,
The scalloped canopy
Of 405 Riverside Drive.
They're singing,
Off-key, but in harmony,
"I knew an old lady
Who swallowed a fly . . ."

"Don't look!"
I almost warn her
And him, too, my son,
Thirty-one
In a grown-up stroller
His mama's pushing.

(At ten,
His hair turned dark like mine,
Curly.
Now . . . the drugs?
The plague?
It's sandy again,
Lank.)

My confidence is shot.
I choke sometimes
At intravenous medication,
Patience,
High curbs.

"Why are we walking in the street?
What's wrong with the sidewalk?
Cars are aiming right for me."

Not only that: the bastards
Have stretched the coming hill
To rise slowly,
Relentlessly,
To a killing length.
I'm not sure I can do it.
"And if you can't?
Will you leave me here?"

We begin to sing,
Off-key, but in harmony,
"I knew an old lady
Who swallowed a fly,
I guess she'll die."

If only.
The old lady.
Me.
Instead of thee.

NOBLE MOTHER

Now I've taken to whining:
Flat on my back again,
I'm close to being fired
Now what?

Now the car is dying,
The handle's off the study door
So we can't get in to where
We store I-V supplies.
Now what?

Now the towel rack's down
In the bathroom,
The dishwasher's puddled
The kitchen floor,
The chairs wobble so
Some medico is sure
To fall through and sue
Like the lawyer next door
Our dog bit.
Now what?

Now I'm afraid
They'll parade some old building code
That forbids loading washers
With laundry like ours.
Now what?

Now on the scene
The armored Nurse Queen
In face mask, gown, and gloves.
I kill her—
In my virulent clothes
Before he's exposed
To full-blown
Fear of plague.
Now what?

Now his veins are shot
And he will not have plumbing
Imbedded inside him
Like sewer lines.
Now what?

Now he's blind in one eye
And almost deaf—
Will they stop at nothing?
He'll be alone soon
Inside AIDS.

And did I say?
The ficus tree is dying.
Good.

INVENTORY

Spastic gait
Deaf
Blind in one eye
No hair
Stiff arm
Battleground
Of the AIDS raids
Still:
Academic gown for bathrobe
Panama hat everywhere
Save flat in bed
And even there:
Shirt
Pants
Shoes
Socks
Belted, buttoned, ready
For a film, a party,
A feast of medieval novels
From Japan
By women, he tells me,
And in the vernacular
Disdained by the men—
Fallow the men.

"Get the car," he says,
"We'll visit your parents."

And when I stall,
Turns quickly away:
"I'll call Patti
We'll try that new place—
The Dead Battery
The Black Hat
Some name like that
Down in Chelsea."

He dials
I hear her machine
The pace is too fast for me.
This must be now, it must be:
There is a new club
That was her machine
Fallow indeed are the men.

But why is he off
To his dead grandparents' house?
And if he's here now,
Thirty-five,
Why does he need me
To drive?

TO THE HONG KONG
DIRECTOR OF REFUGEES

Bobolink, bobolink, BobLien
Such a pretty boy,
Such a lovely voice
How come you're so kind?

Bobolink, bobolink, BobLien
No T cells for years
No symptoms, no tears
How come you're not blind?

Bobolink, bobolink, BobLien
Sickened on Monday
Expired on Friday
How dare you unwind?

Bobolink . . .
Bobolink . . .
Bob Lien . . .
Forgive me
My envy.

RSVP

I didn't raise you to behave this way
I mean, all your pals were here today
Singing, drinking wine . . .
It's been five years, for God's sake,
And you love parties
Couldn't you at least call?

III   *The Card Shop*

He's wanted a sorry-I-haven't-written card
For his sorry friend Elena.
Stubbornly,
Less noble than he,
I've delayed
But today, saw one on Broadway
That's okay,
Given his strange taste
For Hallmark.
Slyly,
I buy it but—
Raked at last awake—
Where we used to sleigh,
Belly-whopping down Dead Man's Hill,
I let the wind off the river
Take it.
I let the wind off the river take it.

EFFECTIVE MOURNING

*For the mourner too will, if asked,
give assurance that the person lost by
death would be happy to know that
the mourner's mind is filled with the
image of the deceased.* *

Of course he wants that.
How else will he stay alive?
In fact, speaking of happy,
I'm happy
When out of the side of my eye
I see his friends cry for him.
Why?
Less work for me
To keep him alive.

Just don't tell me to stop mourning:
"It's what he would want."
Who are you to say
What he would want?
How would you know?

He was no angel
To embrace dying out of turn.

---

*K. Eissler, *Goethe* (Wayne State University Press, 1963), as quoted in
R. Kuhns, *Tragedy* (University of Chicago Press, 1991).

Maybe it's payment he wants,
Sore recompense
From the one who ushered him into life
And then showed him the door.
And does it matter?
Must the living unfailingly follow
The map the dead drew
Though it was found in a backpack
Carefully wrapped in plastic,
Neat in its body bag?

He was always a neat packer
With a messy room.
Claimed nothing could be put away
In this museum display
Of the clothes
Of Robert Henry Mayerson.

Too sassy?
Does the referee
Score a wisecrack
By the deceased
To the keep-him-alive tally?
Does he rack one up for our side,
Grant an indulgence
For the mourner's sly pride?

THE ODDS

You can't replicate love or pain
So experience gets you nowhere.
Love lessons
(If there are any)
Teach only what went wrong
In each case.
With pain, too,
You buy nothing
In those dark stalls
To help you
In the next black hole.
Hard knocks leave marks
That help bad luck
Pick you out.
Don't be fooled:
The distribution of fortune
Isn't random.

ANGELS

Angels are chic again,
Accessorizing AIDS.
I do my part
But the slap of your wings
Against your sides
In the air above me
Makes me too
Fall out laughing.

EXPOSED TO THE AIR

Grief wound me
In fiberglass insulation
Protecting me from common woe
Bloodying me pink to do so.

Thus sheathed,
I saw no predators in the garden,
Heard no lover's rebuff,
Replied to a friend's sorrow
(Though sotto voce)
"You think *that's* bad?"

Now, swaddling wearing thin,
Clever insults harry me
Incorrect bills accrue
Till I snarl
"I'm supposed to put up with this?
After what I've been through?"

(Yet only a fool would imagine
Immunity
To derive from pain,
To thrive
In such bedclothes.)

I DON'T GET IT

When I die, do I win?
Get to thumb my nose
At those whose Notes
From the Pillory
Bury me
In junk mail?

And after he dies at forty-nine
Do I still pine
For the sweetheart
Who grew up to be king?
Do I envy his wife
Her strongbox
Of obits?

And does the girl
Whose rent weeds
Daily chastise me
Miss her mother
More than I
In scarlet cloak
Miss mine?

And will a lingering death
Bring the crowd to its feet
As down the backstretch
The slow track
Gives me
The edge?

And do I lose
The home-court advantage
Old age confers
When my son up and dies
At thirty-five?

And if the plastic bag
Over my head
After I'm dead
Signals the servants
The fix was on . . .
Do I care?

THAT I DON'T
OWN HIS DEATH

That I don't own his death
Is the text
Of a required course
His friends teach:

"I may not be his mother
But you lose your own past
When your first lover dies.
In Seattle,
Under that alley of flowering cherry
I watch for his Chaplin walk,
The cat he trained to 'fetch'
Close behind him,
The tangle of their hair
Gold in the sunlight
As they meander away from me."

"I may not be his mother
But I lost my best friend
And, with him,
The way I saw my own life.
It's in aerobics class
Among the Cobble Hill wives
He takes me over.
I feel my shoulders rise
And my legs go loose

As Robert bops
To Donna Summer's
'Dream Girl.' "

"I may not be his mother
But, like a mother, I fainted
The first time he hung upside down
Outside my dormitory window.
Then, one May night,
That fake Yale fortress
Floodlit by the moon,
He got me to do it
And in that instant
My destiny somersaulted,
I landed in a life
I wouldn't have dared
Without Robert's jubilant lessons."

Stop, stop it now.
Think of how little
Your own mother understands of your life
And you'll feel in your gut
My acid jealousy
As hungrily I force his friends
To speak.

ABOUT THE AUTHOR

Charlotte Mayerson's books include *Home Fires, An Easy Life,* and *Two Blocks Apart.* Her new work of nonfiction, *Goin' to the Chapel,* is to be published in 1996 by Basic Books. Her work has appeared in such magazines as the *Minnesota Review* and *Ms.* Ms. Mayerson's son, Robert Henry Mayerson, the journalist, died on January 2, 1990, of AIDS.